Counting Animals
There Are Four

By Julia Jaske

There are four tigers.

There are four dolphins.

There are four fish.

There are four cheetahs.

There are four elephants.

There are four giraffes.

There are four birds.

There are four pigs.

There are four zebras.

There are four bears.

There are four penguins.

There are four kangaroos.

Word List

tigers	elephants	zebras
dolphins	giraffes	bears
fish	birds	penguins
cheetahs	pigs	kangaroos

14

48 Words

There are four tigers.
There are four dolphins.
There are four fish.
There are four cheetahs.
There are four elephants.
There are four giraffes.
There are four birds.
There are four pigs.
There are four zebras.
There are four bears.
There are four penguins.
There are four kangaroos.

CHERRY BLOSSOM PRESS

Published in the United States of America by Cherry Lake Publishing
Ann Arbor, Michigan
www.cherrylakepublishing.com

Photo Credits: ©Timofeev Vladimir/Shutterstock.com, front cover; ©ArliftAtoz2205/Shutterstock.com, 1; ©Archna Singh/Shutterstock.com, 2; ©Willyam Bradberry/Shutterstock.com, 3; ©TUFADUM/Shutterstock.com, 4; ©Alan Jeffery/Shutterstock.com, 5; ©Villiers Steyn/Shutterstock.com, 6; ©robybenzi/Shutterstock.com, 7; ©Thongchai Pimchan/Shutterstock.com, 8; ©Nadeene/Shutterstock.com, 9; ©nwdph/Shutterstock.com, 10; ©knelson20/Shutterstock.com, 11; ©Moritz Buchty/Shutterstock.com, 12; ©miwa-in-oz/Shutterstock.com, 13; ©StockImageFactory.com/Shutterstock.com, 15

Cherry Blossom Press is an imprint of Cherry Lake Publishing Group.

Library of Congress Cataloging-in-Publication Data
Names: Jaske, Julia, author.
Title: There are four / Julia Jaske.
Description: Ann Arbor, Michigan : Cherry Lake Publishing, 2020. | Series: Counting animals | Audience: Ages 4-6. | Summary: "Look! How many animals do you see? The Counting Animals series uses exciting and familiar animals to support early readers quest to count. The simple text makes it easy for children to engage in reading, and uses the Whole Language approach to literacy, a combination of sight words and repetition that builds recognition and confidence. Bold, colorful photographs correlate directly to the text to help guide readers through the book"— Provided by publisher.
Identifiers: LCCN 2020002989 (print) | LCCN 2020002990 (ebook) | ISBN 9781534168374 (paperback) | ISBN 9781534171893 (pdf) | ISBN 9781534173736 (ebook)
Subjects: LCSH: Counting—Juvenile literature. | Animals—Miscellanea—Juvenile literature.
Classification: LCC QA113 .J397 2020 (print) | LCC QA113 (ebook) | DDC 513.2/1—dc23
LC record available at https://lccn.loc.gov/2020002989
LC ebook record available at https://lccn.loc.gov/2020002990

Cherry Lake Publishing Group would like to acknowledge the work of the Partnership for 21st Century Learning, a Network of Battelle for Kids. Please visit http://www.battelleforkids.org/networks/p21 for more information.

Printed in the United States of America
Corporate Graphics